NATIONAL
GEOGRAPHIC
KiDS

Just Jokes

giggle haha HOWL tee-hee chortle snicker chuckle

591 ½

Rib-Tickling Riddles, Knee-Slapping Knock-Knocks, and Tricky Tongue Twisters for Kids!

NATIONAL GEOGRAPHIC KIDS
NEW YORK

A dino-sour.

**How did the lobster take a
tour of the Grand Canyon?**

By shell-icopter.

Say this fast three times:

Flapjack Jack flipped flat flapjacks.

4

**What do you get if you cross
a turtle and a hedgehog?**

A slowpoke.

**KNOCK!
KNOCK!**
Who's there?
Letters.
Letters who?
Letters in, it's dark out here!

What do you call two spiders who just got married?

Newly-webs.

Chitchat

KID: **Trick or treat!**

WOMAN: **What are you supposed to be?**

KID: **A werewolf.**

WOMAN: **But you aren't wearing a costume.**

KID: **Well, it isn't a full moon yet.**

Why are books about frogs bestsellers?

Because they are quite ribbiting.

Say this fast three times:

Ralph rafts rough rapids.

KNOCK! KNOCK!
Who's there?
Iguana.
Iguana who?
Iguana stop in and say hello.

Hi!

How do you send a secret message in the forest?

By Moss code.

KNOCK! KNOCK!
Who's there?
Cannoli.
Cannoli who?
I cannoli visit for an hour.

6

Why do sponges make the best students?

Because they get absorbed in their schoolwork.

Which people travel the most?

Roam-ans.

What do you call a large Irish spider?

Paddy longlegs.

Chitchat

GINGERBREAD MAN:
I hurt my knee.

GINGERBREAD
WOMAN: **Have you
tried icing it?**

GINGERBREAD MAN:
**Not yet, I've
just been using
a candy cane.**

LAUGHABLE LIST 😆

Crazy campsites:
Camp Soggy Bottom—
leakiest tents around!

Camp Eyedont Wannago—
voted least popular camp
since 2006.

Camp Itchy—we have four
types of bedbugs!

Camp Rickety Pines—you
don't want to set your tent
up under those trees.

**Why did the computer
keep sneezing?**

It had a virus.

Chitchat

JIM: **Want to go rock climbing
with me?**

ELLEN: **I would if I was boulder.**

**What's as sharp as a
vampire's fang?**

The other fang.

Chitchat

CARRIE: **Did you enjoy the tour of the cheese factory?**

CHARLOTTE: **A little bit cheesy, but I thought it was grate! Did you like it?**

CARRIE: **It could have been cheddar.**

8

KNOCK!
KNOCK!
Who's there?
Naan.
Naan who?
**Naan of your business.
Just open the door!**

Which baseball player pours the lemonade?

The pitcher.

How do you stop a canary from calling?

Take away its phone.

Riddle Me THIS!

What's harder to catch the more that you run?

Your breath.

Say this fast three times:

Red bulb, blue bulb.

What do rabbit surgeons perform?

Hop-erations.

Which highway does a tree take on a road trip?

Root 66.

What do you call a guinea pig with four eyes?

Guinea piiig.

KNOCK! KNOCK!
Who's there?
Yeast.
Yeast who?
You could at yeast open the door and say hello!

What did one font say to the other?

"You're just my type!"

Say this fast three times:
Fidgety Philip fidgets frequently.

Say this fast three times:
Slippery slimy slithering snakes slide sideways sometimes.

Why did the student like to take music as her last class?

So she could end the day on a high note.

VEGETABLE FARMER: **My truck has a flat tire.**

SON: **How are we going to fix it?**

VEGETABLE FARMER: **With a-spare-I-guess.**

What did the cyclist eat when he was in last place?

Ketchup.

Riddle Me THIS!

What runs around a haunted house but doesn't move?

A fence.

11

What's a computer's favorite kind of dance?

Disk-o.

Chitchat

SCIENCE TEACHER: **I'd like to have a large whiteboard installed in my classroom.**

PRINCIPAL: **Sure, but what's so great about whiteboards?**

SCIENCE TEACHER: **They're re-markable.**

What does a robot use to shave?

A laser blade.

What did Earth say to the other planets?

"You guys have no life."

What do you get if you cross two snakes and a car window?

Windowshield vipers.

KNOCK! KNOCK!
Who's there?
Foal.
Foal who?
Quit foaling around and get out here.

Why don't computer programmers like nature?

There are too many bugs.

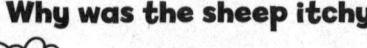

Why was the sheep itchy?

It had fleece.

KNOCK! KNOCK!
Who's there?
Pun.
Pun who?
These jokes could use some punstructive criticism.

What is an egg's favorite horror movie?

The Eggsorcist.

Why did the boy bring lip gloss and eye shadow to school?

He was taking a makeup exam.

What do you get if you cross helium and a monkey?

A hot-air baboon.

Where did the chandelier go to dance?

The Crystal Ball.

What do you get if you cross a rodent and a fruit?

A porcu-pineapple.

Why did the hamburger go to the gym?

It wanted better buns.

What do you get if you cross a flower and a zoo animal?

A rhinoce-rose.

KNOCK! KNOCK!
Who's there?
Kitten.
Kitten who?
I packed everything but the kitten sink for our vacation.

13

What did the polar bear order for lunch?

An iceberg-er.

What do you call an angry grizzly bear?

Furry-ous.

KNOCK! KNOCK!
Who's there?
Sam.
Sam who?
Sam person who knocked on the door the last time!

Why aren't artists good at sports?

Every game ends in a draw.

What did one steak say to the other?

"So we meat again."

Why do people like fountain of youth jokes?

Because they never get old.

Chitchat

PORCUPINE 1: **Do you like my new hat?**
PORCUPINE 2: **Lookin' sharp!**

Say this fast three times:

Five fearless firefighters finally finished the fondue.

What's in the middle of a jellyfish?

A jelly button.

Say this fast three times:

The big beautiful blue balloon burst.

KNOCK! KNOCK!
Who's there?
Water.
Water who?
I just saw your friend, but I don't know water name is.

Riddle Me THIS!

What grows UP while growing down?

A goose.

What is Tarzan's favorite Christmas song?

"Jungle bells."

What kind of medicine do you give a sick bed?

Pill-ows.

Chitchat

DINER: **Oh no! My Hawaiian pizza is burnt!**

WAITER: **Sorry, we should have cooked it at aloha temperature.**

Say this fast three times:

Family financed foreign sci-fi film festival.

Why are kittens good at sports?

Because they are very cat-thletic.

What did the ghost bring its date?

A boo-quet of flowers.

What kind of math does a bird do?

Owl-gebra.

KNOCK! KNOCK!
Who's there?
Filter.
Filter who?
My mom filter pool, so we can go swimming!

What does a monster put in its coffee?

Scream and sugar.

Why was a kitten running an MRI machine?

Because the doctor ordered a CAT scan.

Say this fast three times:

Mark the aardvark went to the park.

Why did the chicken go to the movies?

For hen-tertainment.

Why don't people trust ladders?

Because they're always up to something.

What do you call a hot dog bun with nothing inside it?

A hollow-weenie.

LAUGHABLE LIST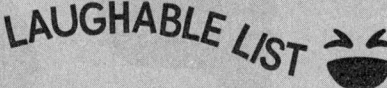

Signs there's a hole in your pool:
You can touch the bottom of the deep end without diving.

Your pool "floaties" become pool "standies."

It takes twice as long to climb out as it did when you climbed in.

Your swimming class turns into a skate-boarding class.

Chitchat

MARATHON RUNNER: I'm here for my pre-race checkup, Doc.

DOCTOR: Well, you seem to be in fantastic condition. Your pulse is like clockwork.

MARATHON RUNNER: That's because your finger is on my watch!

What do chickens do on Sunday afternoons?

They go on peck-nics.

Why is basketball such a messy sport?

Because you dribble on the floor.

What does Dracula take when he is sick?

Bite-amins.

Chitchat

JEFF: What kind of dog finds rare artifacts?

ERIN: A bark-eologist.

JEFF: How does it find them?

ERIN: It digs them up.

Why couldn't the trout get money out of the ATM?

He had insuf-fish-ent funds.

Does it cost a lot of money to buy an insect?

Not if they're free-bees!

Who won the skeleton beauty pageant?

Nobody.

Chitchat

EYE DOCTOR: Eye see it's time for your appointment.

PATIENT: Iris you didn't make such a bad pun.

EYE DOCTOR: Sorry my joke was so cornea.

What was the baker's favorite movie?

Indiana Scones.

What does an aardvark like on its pizza?

Ant-chovies.

Say this fast three times:

Ghosts host roasts on coats.

What do they serve for lunch at martial arts camp?

Kung food.

What did one toilet say to the other?

"You look a bit flushed."

What do you call an elephant in a kayak?

Stuck.

What is a dentist's favorite animal?

A molar bear.

What is a cat's favorite TV show?

Claw and Order.

KNOCK! KNOCK!
Who's there?
Pasta.
Pasta who?
I walked right pasta house.

Why did the sick girl go to the shoemaker?

So she could be heeled.

How did the cheddar cheese feel after its vacation?

It felt grate!

Did you hear about the famous pickle?

He's a really big dill!

Riddle Me THIS!

A baseball team won 5-0 but not a single man ran around the bases. How is that possible?

All the men were married.

Why did the teacher bring birdseed to school?

She had a parrot-teacher conference.

Which flag do monkeys wave on the Fourth of July?

The star-spangled banana.

How did the burger propose to the French fry?

With an onion ring.

What do you call a potato that joins a monastery?

A chip-monk.

Chitchat

ELEPHANT 1: Hey, can I talk to you about something?

ELEPHANT 2: I'm all ears!

Why did the boy who never played basketball decide to join a team?

He wanted to give it a shot.

What's the hardest part about skydiving?

The ground.

What kind of shoes do alligators wear?

Crocs.

Say this fast three times:

Six sharp smart sharks.

What did the nose say to the cold?

"Catch ya later!"

Who do monsters buy cookies from?

The Ghoul Scouts.

KNOCK!
KNOCK!
Who's there?
Neon.
Neon who?
I fell and hurt my neon the pavement.

What do you call a bee that
can't make up its mind?

A maybee.

LAUGHABLE LIST

Lesser known landmarks:
Bonehenge—it's really just a pile of bones
behind a hot wing restaurant.

The Kinda OK Canyon—not as impressive as
that other one.

Statue of Bitter Tea—paying tribute to the
world's worst hot drink.

Great Wall of Saliva—just stay home.

Riddle Me THIS!

What SITS when it stands and jumps when it walks?

A kangaroo.

Why did the teacher wear sunglasses on her school trip?

Because her students were so bright.

KNOCK!
KNOCK!
Who's there?
Sand.
Sand who?
Sand me a text when you are ready to leave.

Why do geologists make the best guitarists?

Because they know how to rock!

Chitchat

CUSTOMER: **So do you like being a baker?**

BAKER: **Sure do, it's a piece of cake!**

What do you get if you cross a van and an elephant?

A vehicle with extra trunk space.

How does Darth Vader like his toast?

On the dark side.

What happened to the cat that swallowed a ball of yarn?

She had mittens.

Say this fast three times:

Rosie runs rapidly in the rain.

Chitchat

MARIE: **Did you cut the grass today?**

GARY: **No, I just didn't feel mow-tivated.**

What's worse than raining cats and dogs?

Hailing taxis.

29

Chitchat

CHEF: **How did you enjoy the soup?**

DINER: **It was stew-pendous!**

Yum!

Why was the teenager so sad when his camera broke?

Because he couldn't picture himself without it.

Say this fast three times:

Bamboo baboon.

What does a dentist call his x-rays?

Tooth-pics.

What did the chef give her husband for Valentine's Day?

A hug and a quiche.

KNOCK!
KNOCK!
Who's there?
Swimmer.
Swimmer who?
Hey, swimmer down. No need to yell.

What do you get if you cross a lifeguard and a computer?

A screen saver.

How do you teach a puppy to walk down the stairs?

Step by step.

Say this fast three times:

Three-toed tree toad.

Why did the pig drop out of the marathon?

Because it pulled a hamstring.

Ouch!

Signs you have an old computer:
You have to crank a handle to start it.

___

The screen is made by Etch A Sketch.

___

It's connected to the internet by a piece of string and a tin can.

___

Your messaging app is a carrier pigeon.

Why are piemakers so well prepared?

Because they always have a flan B.

What's green, has eight legs, and comes with chips?

A guactopus.

What do you call a nut with facial hair?

A mustachio.

What do you get if you cross an insect and a precious jewel?

A rubee.

Say this fast three times:

A biscuit mixer mixes mixed biscuits.

Where do monkeys get all their gossip?

Through the grapevine.

Chitchat

DAVID: **I just don't understand how gems are formed.**

LAUREN: **Really? It's crystal clear to me!**

What quacks and has feathers and fangs?

Count Duckula.

KNOCK! KNOCK!
Who's there?
Butternut.
Butternut who?
Butternut be late for the movie.

Say this fast three times:

Eleven excited elves exchanged expensive earrings.

What do you get if you cross a Halloween treat and a mythical creature?

Uni-candy-corn.

What's green and snuggly?

An avo-cuddle.

Say this fast three times:

A skunk thunk the stump stunk.

How do you arrest a pig?

Put him in ham-cuffs.

Chitchat

IRON 1: **I need to speak with you immediately!**

IRON 2: **Is it a pressing matter?**

KNOCK! KNOCK!
Who's there?
Hugo.
Hugo who?
Hugo to the store and I'll stay home.

KNOCK! KNOCK!
Who's there?
Wader.
Wader who?
Wader, there's a fly in my soup.

What do computers eat for a snack?

Microchips.

Say this fast three times:

Santa's short suit shrank.

What kind of beans won't grow in your garden?

Jelly beans.

Chitchat

STATUE 1: **Do you like my new outfit?**

STATUE 2: **Wow! You look marble-ous!**

Why did the tiny pepper put on a sweater?

She was a little chili.

What do you get if you cross a snake and a piece of fruit?

A banana-conda.

Which is the noisiest sport?

Racket-ball.

Why did the polar bear call tech support from the North Pole?

Because his computer was frozen.

What has a

NECK

35

but no

head?

36

A bottle.

What do computers do on first dates?

Grab a byte.

What kind of shoe does a ghost wear?

Booooots.

Chitchat

FISHERMAN 1: **Is this river good for fish?**

FISHERMAN 2: **It must be. I can't get any of them to leave.**

What did the biologist buy at the high-end boutique?

Designer genes.

Who do dogs hire to design doghouses?

A bark-itect.

Chitchat

TONY: **Why did you put glasses on your cell phone?**

LOUISE: **Because it lost its contacts.**

What happens to skydivers when it rains?

They get wet.

KNOCK! KNOCK!
Who's there?
Wheat.
Wheat who?
Wheat a second—this is the wrong house!

What kind of pastry comes from Britain?

An English muffin.

What did the pencil say to the paper?

"I dot my eye on you."

What does a bird say when it feels bad about something?

"My apologeese."

How do cars greet each other?

With their hi beams.

KNOCK! KNOCK!
Who's there?
Wire.
Wire who?
Wire you asking?
I just told you.

What do birds use when skydiving?

Sparrow-chutes.

Why did the patient with amnesia go for a run?

To jog her memory.

KNOCK! KNOCK!
Who's there?
Bee.
Bee who?
Bee-ware, there's a full moon tonight.

Why did the ferret say "moo"?

It was learning a new language.

Why did the invisible man turn down a free kayaking trip?

He just couldn't see himself doing it.

Chitchat

CUTLERY 1: **Have a knife day!**

CUTLERY 2: **See you spoon!**

KNOCK! KNOCK!
Who's there?
Canoe.
Canoe who?
Canoe open this door? I'm tired of knocking.

What do you call the horse next door?

Your neigh-bor.

What do you call a turtle wearing a scarf?

Cold.

What is a marsupial's favorite soft drink?

Coca-Koala.

How can you tell if a cat has been using your computer?

There are teeth marks
on your mouse.

How do rabbits travel?

By hare-plane.

What do you call a doctor who fixes websites?

A URL-ologist.

KNOCK!
KNOCK!
Who's there?
Sweeter.
Sweeter who?
Can I borrow a sweeter? It's chilly.

KNOCK! KNOCK!
Who's there?
Ooze.
Ooze who?
Ooze that monster creeping up on you?!

Why did the dachshund put ketchup on himself?

Because someone called him a hot dog!

What do you call a hiker's playlist?

A trail mix.

Where do royal corgis live?

In Barkingham Palace.

Where does a cruise ship go when it's not feeling well?

To the dock-tor.

KNOCK! KNOCK!
Who's there?
Butter.
Butter who?
You butter be ready to go!

What happened when the ape walked into the ice-cream parlor?

The banana split.

KNOCK! KNOCK!
Who's there?
Al dente.
Al dente who?
I don't want to knock too hard. I'm afraid al dente the door.

What is a ghost's favorite holiday?

April Ghouls' Day.

How do trees feel in the springtime?

Re-leaved.

Which Renaissance painter had a sweet tooth?

Donut-ello.

KNOCK! KNOCK!
Who's there?
Ogre.
Ogre who?
Thought I'd come ogre for a visit.

What do dogs order in restaurants?

Paw-sta.

KNOCK! KNOCK!
Who's there?
Llama.
Llama who?
Llama take a selfie before we go.

What advice did the blood bank manager have for her staff?

B positive. This job can be draining.

Why did the cookie go to the doctor after hiking?

Because it was feeling crumby.

KNOCK! KNOCK!
Who's there?
Jamaican.
Jamaican who?
Jamaican dinner? I'm starving.

**What do snowmen
eat for breakfast?**

Snowflakes.

Why are fish terrible tennis players?

They don't like getting close to the net.

**What string instrument
does a ghost play?**

A BOO-kulele.

What kind of pie can fly?

A magpie.

What travels **around the world** but never leaves its **corner?**

45

46

A stamp.

How do French fries get to work?

On their fry-cycles.

Chitchat

SAFARI TOURIST: Is it hard to spot a leopard?

SAFARI GUIDE: No, they come that way.

What did the cell phone say to the phone charger?

"I'd die without you."

How does a statue call home?

On its iStone.

What does a superhero put in their iced tea?

Just-ice.

What kind of dinosaur could do magic?

A *Tyrannosaurus hex*.

48

Chitchat

SKIER 1: **I can't find my sister. She was just near the chairlift.**

SKIER 2: **She's gondola top of the mountain.**

Where does a shrimp go to sell its jewelry?

The prawn-shop.

What do witches order at fancy hotels?

Broom service.

What kind of dog doesn't bark?

A hush puppy.

**KNOCK!
KNOCK!**
Who's there?
Queso.
Queso who?
**I've got a bad queso
the sniffles.**

**What time is it
when Godzilla sits
on your bed?**

Time to get a
new bed.

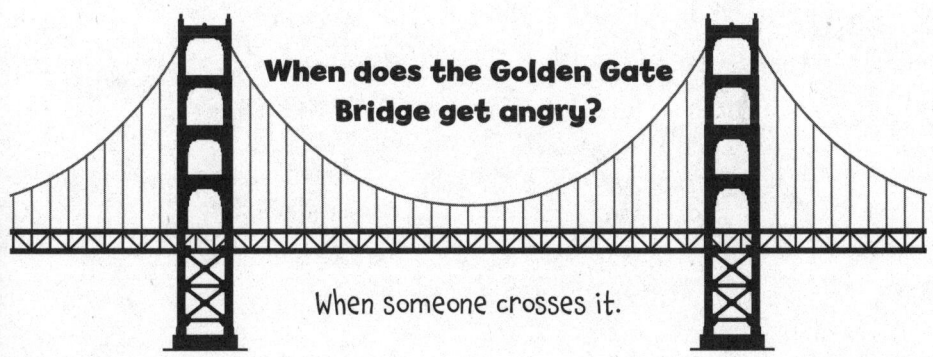

**When does the Golden Gate
Bridge get angry?**

When someone crosses it.

**What do you call
a cow that
doesn't give milk?**

An udder failure.

**KNOCK!
KNOCK!**
Who's there?
Shell.
Shell who?
Shell we leave now?

**Where do rabbits
go after they get
married?**

On their bunnymoon.

Who will fix your
cavity if your dentist
is on vacation?

Whoever is filling in.

KNOCK!
KNOCK!
Who's there?
Ivory.
Ivory who?
**Ivory now and then
I like to stop by.**

**What's worse than
having a snake in your
sleeping bag?**

Two snakes in your
sleeping bag.

**What did the
ghost cook for her
dinner party?**

Ghoulash.

Why is it hard to talk to a goat?

Because they're always butting in.

What do you get if you teach a spotted cat to sing?

A show leopard.

What's green and jumpy?

A grasshopper with the hiccups.

Say this fast three times:

Chop shops stock chops.

What happened to the corn when it didn't do its homework?

It got an earful from the teacher.

How did the barber win the cross-country race?

He took a shortcut.

What do cat journalists report on?

Breaking mews.

Where did the sheep get his hair cut?

At the baabaa shop.

Say this fast three times:

Selfish shellfish.

Chitchat

MANAGER: There's a broken bottle of oil in aisle two.

EMPLOYEE: How much of it spilled?

MANAGER: Olive it.

EMPLOYEE: I canola imagine how long it will take to clean up.

Did you hear about the wooden car with the wooden engine?

It wooden go.

KNOCK! KNOCK!
Who's there?
Pollen.
Pollen who?
Are you pollen my leg?

What do you call a member of the weasel family that likes to knit?

A wool-verine.

What did the cupcake do on vacation?

Muffin much.

Say this fast three times:

Valerie's hourly salary.

Why won't the baker share her bread recipe with anyone?

She says it's on a knead-to-know basis.

What happened to the ox who bought his wife chocolates on Valentine's Day?

He became more love-a-bull.

What do you call a gossipy monkey?

A blab-oon.

Chitchat

STUDENT 1: **I'm taking French, Spanish, and algebra this year.**

STUDENT 2: **How do you say "good evening" in algebra?**

Say this fast three times:

Cheap ship trips.

What do you call a loaf of bread acting silly?

A weirdough.

KNOCK! KNOCK!
Who's there?
Herd.
Herd who?
Herd you were home—want to come out and play?

How do fleas travel?

They go itch-hiking.

What do ghosts use to clean their hair?

Sham-boo!

Say this fast three times:

Cucumber cummerbund.

Why shouldn't you play football with a pig?

Because he'll hog the ball.

What do you call a grumpy ex-hockey player?

No more Mr. Ice Guy.

Why do cows wear bells around their necks?

Because their horns don't work.

Where do hogs look up the meaning of words?

The pigtionary.

At what school do you have to **DROP OUT** in order to **graduate?**

55

Skydiving school.

Why were the two bridges fighting?

Because they were arch enemies.

LAUGHABLE LIST 😆

Animal Valentine's Day cards:

Octopus—I ink I love you.

Deer—I'm very fawned of you.

Dinosaur—I'm raptor round your finger.

Wildebeest—I gnu you were the one for me.

Snake—I hiss you were here.

What kind of fruit should you call if you lock yourself out of the house?

A key-wi.

What do you say to a rodent when it leaves for work?

Have a mice day!

58

KNOCK! KNOCK!
Who's there?
Woo.
Woo who?
Wow! You are really excited to have visitors!

What kind of vehicle does Bigfoot drive?

A monster truck.

Chitchat

GHOUL: **Why do you think we get along so well?**

DEMON: **Because demons are a ghoul's best friend!**

Where do fish go on vacation?

Finland.

How do birds keep their sneakers on?

With Velcrow.

How do sweater-makers come up with new patterns?

They imagine knit.

What do you get if you cross a Scottish monster and a German cheese?

The Loch Ness Muenster.

What kind of food should you eat at the seashore?

Pier-ogi.

KNOCK! KNOCK!
Who's there?
Julian.
Julian who?
Just Julian—there is no one else with me.

Why do puppies make the best kayakers?

Because they are natural dog paddlers.

Where do fish professors teach?

Tunaversity.

How do astronauts serve dinner?

In satellite dishes.

What do you get if you cross a puppy and a frog?

A dog that can lick you from the other side of the yard.

Why do computer programmers have terrible table manners?

Because they take mega-bites.

KNOCK! KNOCK!
Who's there?
Tennis.
Tennis who?
Tennis five plus five.

Chitchat

ASHA: **Are you going to teach your dog to play soccer?**

ADITYA: **Of course not—he's a boxer!**

KNOCK! KNOCK!
Who's there?
Hive.
Hive who?
Hive been out here for ages!

What's the difference between bird flu and swine flu?

One requires tweetment and the other needs oinkment.

Why do polar bears have fur coats?

Because they would look silly in sweaters.

Why do people whisper in the pharmacy?

So they don't wake the sleeping pills.

What do you call a piece of fruit that needs glasses?

Visually im-peared.

Why did the orange join the navy?

Because it was a naval orange.

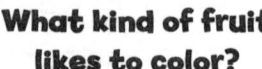

What kind of fruit likes to color?

A crayonberry.

Where is the best place to try new bubblegum?

On a chew chew train.

Why are horses so calm under pressure?

Because they come from a stable environment.

62

What do you get if you cross a pie and an ape?

A meringue-utan.

Chitchat

DOG 1: **Want to hear a knock-knock joke?**

DOG 2: **Sure!**

DOG 1: **Knock, kno—**

DOG 2: **BARK, BARK!**

What do you call the slowest competitor in a downhill ski race?

A slope-poke.

KNOCK!
KNOCK!
Who's there?
Swarm.
Swarm who?
Swarm today, isn't it?

**Where do lambs share
their videos?**

On Ewe-Tube.

**What do you call a
porcelain knight?**

Sir-amic.

**KNOCK!
KNOCK!**
Who's there?
Scone.
Scone who?
**Come to the park.
It's scone to be fun.**

**Did you hear about the
fruit truck that crashed
on the highway?**

It created a traffic jam.

Why did the chicken cross the basketball court?

Because the ref called a fowl.

What did one magnet say to the other?

"I find you very attractive."

How do hedgehogs hug each other?

Very, very carefully.

Why won't you find cattle at scary movies?

Because they are cow-ards.

A **HORSE** is tied to a 10-foot **ROPE.** There is a bale of hay 20 feet away from him, but the horse **can still eat from it.** How is that possible?

65

The other end of the rope isn't tied to anything.

Where did the carpenter buy his measuring stick?

At a yard sale.

Chitchat

ALLISON: I used to have a fear of hurdles.

DIEGO: How did you get over it?

What do you get if you cross a giraffe and a hedgehog?

A six-foot-long toothbrush.

What's the difference between a dog and a marine biologist?

One wags a tail and the other tags a whale.

LAUGHABLE LIST

Pig party games:

Bobbing for Slop

Pin the Tail on the Farmer

Duck Duck Goose Cow Chicken Pony Goat ...

Hogscotch

What did the tornado say to the car?

"Want to go for a spin?"

KNOCK! KNOCK!
Who's there?
Fangs.
Fangs who?
Fangs for inviting me over.

Which is a witch's favorite subject?

Spell-ing.

KNOCK! KNOCK!
Who's there?
Voodoo.
Voodoo who?
Voodoo you think?

Why did the food taster quit her job?

Because she had too much on her plate.

Why aren't sumo wrestlers friends with race-car drivers?

Because they move in different circles.

Chitchat

ROBOT: **You always make me so angry!**

LAB TECH: **I know how to push your buttons.**

What happened when the girl tried to catch fog in a jar?

She mist.

What do you get if you cross a creek and a river?

Wet feet.

What kind of insects bother musicians?

Flute flies.

Chitchat

BOB: **I can cut a piece of wood in half just by looking at it.**

DOUG: **No you can't!**

BOB: **It's true. I saw it with my own eyes.**

Why is a jaguar so good at trivia?

Because every guess is spot-on.

What do archers wear when they want to get dressed up?

Bow ties.

What do you call a monster with no neck?

The Lost Neck Monster.

KNOCK! KNOCK!
Who's there?
Squidding.
Squidding who?
You've got to be squidding me right now!

What do you get if you cross a musical instrument and a snorkeler?

A tuba diver.

What did one pumpkin say to the other pumpkin?

"Hey there, gourd-geous!"

Why is tennis such a loud game?

Because each player raises a racket.

KNOCK! KNOCK!
Who's there?
Santa.
Santa who?
Santa card to you last week. Did you get it yet?

Why did the robot take a vacation?

To recharge his batteries.

What do cats put in their soft drinks?

Mice cubes.

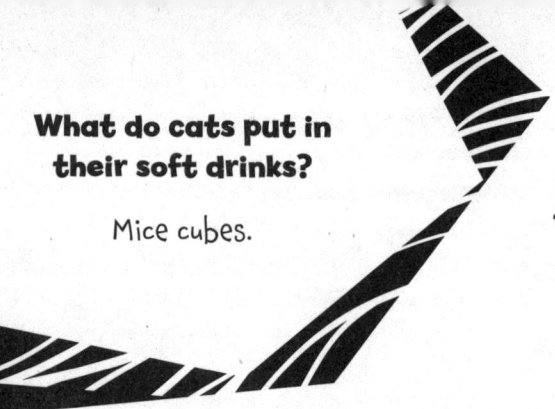

Why didn't the girl take the bus home from her camping trip?

Because her mom would make her bring it back.

What kind of music do chefs play in the kitchen?

Wok-and-roll.

KNOCK! KNOCK!
Who's there?
Ida.
Ida who?
Ida emailed but I have no Wi-Fi connection.

What's the difference between a jeweler and a jailer?

One sells watches and the other watches cells.

Why was the dairy farmer limping?

Because he sprained his calf.

What did the schnauzer say to the hot dog bun?

"Are you a pure-bread?"

What do you call a pig from Ontario?
Canadian bacon.

Why did the Dalmatian refuse to bathe in dishwasher detergent?

He didn't want to come out spotless.

KNOCK! KNOCK!
Who's there?
Some fin.
Some fin who?
Some fin tells me this is another knock-knock joke.

73

What oinks and tells you the weather forecast?

A ham radio.

Say this fast three times:
Four fine fillies flitted their forelocks.

What do pine trees wear to the lake?

Swimming trunks.

What do spirits send home while on vacation?

Ghost-cards.

What did the sink say to the water faucet?

"You're a real drip."

Why didn't the girl get rid of her pet leech?

Because she was really attached to it.

Why can't you trick an x-ray technician?

Because they can always see through you.

What kind of workouts do chickens follow?

Eggs-ercise routines.

How does the Abominable Snowman build his house?

Igloos it together.

Say this fast three times:

Sasquatch's squashed watches.

Why don't cats like dog jokes?

Because they are pawful.

Chitchat

GARY: **Did you hear that the invisible man married the invisible woman and they had a baby?**

NICO: **Is the baby cute?**

GARY: **She's not much to look at.**

Say this fast three times:

Brian from Britain has bitten my mitten.

What holiday do condiments celebrate?

Cinco de Mayo!

What can you find in the middle of the ocean?

The letter e.

Who can shave 10 times a day and still have a beard?

A barber.

Where do penguins keep their money?

In a snowbank.

What kind of dinosaur loves English class?

A thesaurus.

Chitchat

MOM COW: **It's time for bed!**

CALF: **Do I calf to go?**

MOM COW: **Yes, it's pasture bedtime.**

What lights up a stadium?

A soccer match.

What do witches use to style their hair?

Scare spray.

Why do scuba divers fall off the boat backward to enter the water?

Because if they fell forward, they'd fall in the boat.

Chitchat

PATIENT: **I think I was bitten by a vampire.**

DOCTOR: **Take a drink of water.**

PATIENT: **Will it make me better?**

DOCTOR: **No, but I'll be able to see if your neck leaks.**

What kind of money do fishermen make?

Net profits.

**KNOCK!
KNOCK!**
Who's there?
Adelia.
Adelia who?
**Adelia cards and we can
play Go Fish!**

What activity does the sun enjoy?

Solar-blading.

Where do mice park their boats?

At the hickory dickory dock.

Chitchat

CUSTOMER: **How much is that duck?**

PET STORE OWNER: **Ten dollars.**

CUSTOMER: **OK, could you please send me the bill?**

PET STORE OWNER: **I'm sorry, but you'll have to take the whole bird.**

Why did the coffee beans go to jail?

Because there were grounds for arrest.

What kind of street does a ghost live on?

A dead end.

Why are petri dishes so smart?

Because they're very cultured.

Which race is never run?

A swimming race.

What is Bigfoot's favorite month?

Oc-toe-ber.

What do you get if you cross a magician and a dog?

A Labracadabrador.

LAUGHABLE LIST

New dog breeds:
Collie + Lhasa apso = collapso—folds up to fit into small doghouses.

German shepherd + cocker spaniel = shocker—a dog that's always surprising you.

Collie + malamute = comute—you have to travel a long way to find one.

Afghan + Labrador retriever = Afghan retriever—brings you a blanket.

Shar-pei + German pointer = sharp point—be careful when petting this one.

What do you get if you cross a soft drink and a robot?

A can-droid.

What happened when the potato chip factory caught fire?

It burned to a crisp.

What did the bug say when it hit the windshield?

"I don't have the guts to do that again."

KNOCK! KNOCK!
Who's there?
Amos.
Amos who?
Amos-quito landed on my nose!

Where do vampires keep their Easter eggs?

In their Easter caskets.

KNOCK! KNOCK!
Who's there?
Nickel.
Nickel who?
Nickel be dropping by for a visit later.

What did the sardine call the submarine tour?

A can of people.

What happened when the werewolf swallowed a clock?

He got ticks.

What's a pirate's favorite letter?

You'd think it's *r* but it be the *c*.

KNOCK!
KNOCK!
Who's there?
Acid.
Acid who?
Acid open the door!

What do you call it when a teacher falls off a bus?

A school trip.

Which fish only comes out at night?

A sea star.

KNOCK! KNOCK!
Who's there?
Cashew.
Cashew who?
Give me all the cashew have.

How did the flashlight feel when its batteries died?

It was delighted.

Why do dogs like to wear hats?

Because they look quite fetching.

What happens if you wear a snowsuit inside?

It melts.

What do you call a pet snake that can't sit still?

Viper-active.

Why isn't tanning a competitive sport?

Because you can only get bronze.

How many oranges grow on a tree?

All of them.

KNOCK! KNOCK!
Who's there?
Kanga.
Kanga who?
No, it's called a kangaROO.

What do you get if you cross a fishing lure and an old gym sock?

A hook, line, and stinker.

KNOCK! KNOCK!
Who's there?
Snow.
Snow who?
Snow time to lose! Let's get moving!

Which season is the best time to trampoline?

Springtime.

Why do musicians make people laugh?

Because their jokes are pretty sharp.

**KNOCK!
KNOCK!**
Who's there?
Havana.
Havana who?
We're Havana good time!

**What do you call a
small loaf of bread that
makes a great mentor?**

A roll model.

**Where can you
learn all about
chickens?**

In the hencyclopedia.

**What do you get if you cross a
carnival ride and a weasel?**

A Ferret wheel.

What kind of cars do kittens drive?

Cat-illacs.

Why did the opera singer go sailing?

She wanted to hit the high C's.

What has large fangs and says "baa"?

A ram-pire.

Chitchat

MONSTER 1: **What is your son studying at medical school?**

MONSTER 2: **Nothing, they're studying him!**

What kind of animal loves to eat bread?

A carbavore.

Why did the comedian stop at the fabric store?

He was looking for new material.

What do you call a surprised turtle?

Shell-shocked.

Chitchat

ELLEN: **How do you like your soft drink?**

JIM: **It is soda-licious!**

Why can't snails play together nicely?

Because they always slug each other.

KNOCK! KNOCK!
Who's there?
Safari.
Safari who?
Safari, so good.

Why did the fish get embarrassed?

Because it saw the ocean's bottom.

Why did the kid sleep on a battery?

She needed a power nap.

What do vampires take for a sore throat?

Coffin drops.

Chitchat

ZOOKEEPER 1: **Why did you measure this snake in inches?**

ZOOKEEPER 2: **Because they don't have feet.**

Say this fast three times:

Round the rugged rocks the ragged rascals ran.

KNOCK! KNOCK!
Who's there?
Chicken.
Chicken who?
I'd like to chicken to my room, please.

Which contest did the broom win?

The sweepstakes.

What kind of car does an insect drive?

A Volkswagen Beetle.

85

Say this fast three times:

Gritty witty city kitty.

Chitchat

PARAKEET 1: **Is it hot out today?**

PARAKEET 2: **I didn't check the feather forecast.**

Why did the orange stop climbing halfway up the mountain?

It ran out of juice.

How do you stop a charging rhinoceros?

Take away his credit card.

What kind of lunch do you get in the desert?

Sand-wiches.

Chitchat

WAITER ON A CRUISE SHIP: **Would you like to see a menu, sir?**

WEREWOLF: **No thanks, just bring me the passenger list.**

What is a scarecrow's favorite fruit?

Straw-berries.

Why do zombies make great employees?

Because they are dead-icated.

What do you get if you cross a robot and a gardener?

Cutting-hedge technology.

What
has to be
BROKEN
before you can
use it?

87

An egg.

What sparkles and hops?

A kanga-ruby.

What do you get if you cross a slice of bread and a bloodsucking bug?

Mosqui-toast.

Say this fast three times:

Haunted houses house horrifying haunts.

Say this fast three times:

Five frantic frogs fled from fifty fierce fishes.

What do you call a baby monkey that's similar to its dad?

A chimp off the old block.

What's big and hairy and has three wheels?

Bigfoot on a tricycle.

KNOCK! KNOCK!
Who's there?
Bear claws.
Bear claws who?
I'm knocking bear claws I want to come in!

Chitchat
MARIA: **I can't find my rutabaga!**

WENDY: **Don't worry, it will turnip!**

How can you tell if the tree you are camping under is a dogwood?

By the bark.

KNOCK! KNOCK!
Who's there?
Nacho.
Nacho who?
This is nacho house! Get outta here quick!

Which ghost is the best dancer?

The boogie-man.

KNOCK! KNOCK!
Who's there?
Zombies.
Zombies who?
Zombies make honey; zombies don't.

KNOCK! KNOCK!
Who's there?
Taco.
Taco who?
Open the door and we can taco 'bout it.

What kind of lock does a ghost have on its front door?

A dead bolt.

Chitchat

FARMER 1: **Why does this chicken coop only have two doors?**

FARMER 2: **Because if it had four doors it would be a sedan.**

Why did the witches' team lose the baseball game?

Their bats flew away.

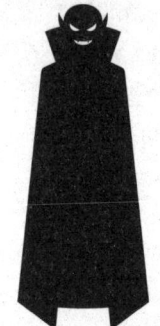

Terrible safari advertisements:

Ever wanted to smell a rhino's breath?

The world's first walking tour of Lion's Cove!

Run with the wildebeests!

Tour Leopard's Lair—the first 10 bandages are free!

Chitchat

92

DRACULA: **I'd like to write a book about my life.**

GHOUL: **Maybe you should find a ghostwriter.**

DRACULA: **I'm hoping it will be a bestseller.**

GHOUL: **Then you can start a fang club!**

Why was the computer tired when it got home?

Because it had a hard drive.

What do you call a girl hanging onto a basketball hoop?

Annette.

Chitchat

MOM: **I'm going to tell you a story about a haunted refrigerator.**

DAUGHTER: **That sounds chilling!**

KNOCK!
KNOCK!
Who's there?
Scold.
Scold who?
Scold enough out here for ice-skating.

Why do cats like going to spas?

They enjoy being pam-purred.

What happened when the chemist tried to tell a joke?

She didn't get a reaction.

Chitchat

WRITER: **I think I have writer's block.**

EDITOR: **Why don't you head to the cemetery? There's lots of plots there.**

KNOCK!
KNOCK!
Who's there?
Weirdo.
Weirdo who?
Weirdo you keep your Halloween costumes?

Where does a ghoul water-ski?

On Lake Eerie.

What kind of animals will you find working at a print shop?

Copycats that make paw prints.

KNOCK! KNOCK!
Who's there?
Quack.
Quack who?
Quack another bad joke and I'm leaving.

Say this fast three times:

Llamas lying lazily aloft a little log.

LAUGHABLE LIST

Signs you're in a bad motel:
You have to wait for the person next door to be done with the towel so you can use it.

The complimentary newspaper tells you that the United States finally landed on the moon.

The mint on the pillow runs away from you when you try to pick it up.

There is fuzzy brown stuff on the floor, but the manager insists none of the rooms are carpeted.

A family of cockroaches posted a negative review on the motel's website.

How can you tell when a doughnut is daydreaming?

Its eyes are glazed over.

What do you call it when two pigs jump out and surprise you?

A hambush.

KNOCK! KNOCK!

Who's there?

Loafing.

Loafing who?

I'm loafing my head off at these jokes.

What does Canada produce that no other country produces?

Canadians.

Chitchat

VAMPIRE 1: **What did you think of that Dracula movie?**

VAMPIRE 2: **It was fang-tastic!**

What do you call a zombie that is pressing your doorbell?

A dead ringer.

LAUGHABLE LIST

Books by robot authors:

Artificial Intelligence and You by Anne Droid

Don't Lose Your Head: A Guide to Keeping It Together by Si Borg

---

If I Only Had a Heart by Otto Maton

How to Keep Your Insides Ticking by Olata Gears

A Guide to Heavy Metal Music by Metal Hedz

Chitchat

FARMER 1: **Who raided my vegetable patch?**

FARMER 2: **Beets me!**

Why can't skeletons play church music?

Because they don't have organs.

Chitchat

JULIA: **I was going to teach my turtle to ride a bike, but I changed my mind.**

CATHIE: **Why?**

JULIA: **Because he doesn't have a thumb to ring the bell.**

Why do gymnasts make the best friends?

Because they always bend over backward for people.

Chitchat

COW 1: **Hey, who's the new calf?**

COW 2: **I don't know. I've never seen herbivore.**

What do you call it when you are scared by the same ghost twice?

Déjà boo.

A man rode into the Grand Canyon on **Friday,** stayed for two nights, and left on Friday. How is this **possible?**

97

His mule's name
was Friday.

KNOCK!
KNOCK!
Who's there?
Bubbly.
Bubbly who?
**I'm prob-bubbly going
shopping, wanna come?**

Chitchat

DUCK: **Who's paying for dinner tonight?**

SKUNK: **I don't have a scent.**

DEER: **I don't have a buck to spare.**

DUCK: **I guess we'll just put it on my bill.**

KNOCK!
KNOCK!
Who's there?
Cook.
Cook who?
**Stop making bird noises and
open the door!**

What kind of scientist needs a tan?

A pale-eontologist.

Why did the hot dog lose the race?

Because he couldn't ketchup. But don't worry, he mustard the strength to try again!

KNOCK! KNOCK!

Who's there?

Classify.

Classify who?

Classify promise no homework, will you please pay attention?

100

Chitchat

SANJIDA: **Oh no, 500 hares have escaped from the zoo!**

PRIYA: **Don't worry, the police are combing the area.**

SANJIDA: **I hope every-bunny gets home safe.**

KNOCK!
KNOCK!
Who's there?
Shave.
Shave who?
Shave the jokes for later.
Let's get going!

How are colds like bad criminals?

Because they are easy to catch.

What do you call two raspberries playing guitars?

A jam session.

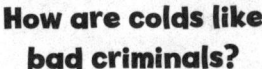

KNOCK!
KNOCK!
Who's there?
Latte.
Latte who?
It's beginning to look a latte like Christmas.

KNOCK!
KNOCK!
Who's there?
Frappé.
Frappé who?
Frappé birthday to you!

Why did the man marry a barbecue?

Because it was the grill of his dreams.

Say this fast three times:

Sloppy Slurpees.

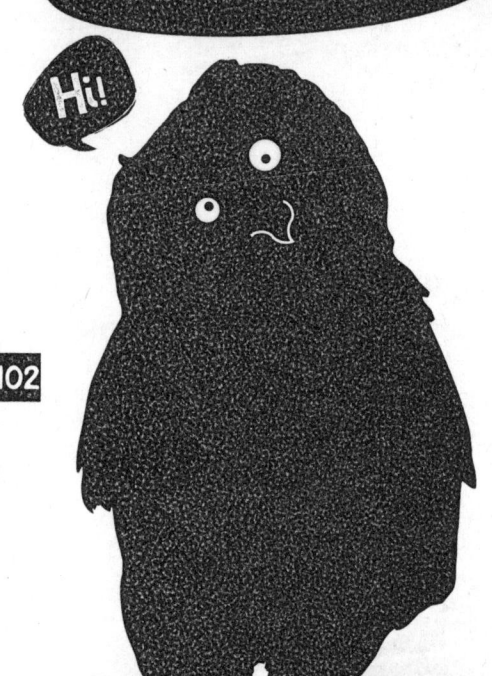

Hi!

KNOCK!
KNOCK!
Who's there?
Bed.
Bed who?
Bed you can't guess who this is!

Say this fast three times:

Chester chews a chunk of cheap cheddar cheese.

KNOCK!
KNOCK!
Who's there?
Owl.
Owl who?
Owl wait for you in the car.

What's green and barks?

Broc-collie.

102

What kind of car does a baker drive?

A hy-bread.

Riddle Me THIS!

It comes in only one color, but many different sizes. It lives where there's light, but will die in the dark. What is it?

Your shadow.

Say this fast three times:

Sam snapped a selfie on a silver cell phone.

103

What is a hog's favorite type of cookie?

Pig Newtons.

Riddle Me THIS!

Which animal wears a coat in the winter and pants in the summer?

A dog.

KNOCK! KNOCK!
Who's there?
Crumb.
Crumb who?
I'm hoping you'll crumb to your senses.

How does a skeleton call her friends?

On the tele-bone.

Chitchat

ALVARO: **I'm learning to surf in my kitchen.**

KAI: **Where?**

ALVARO: **On the micro-wave!**

KNOCK! KNOCK!
Who's there?
Whisker.
Whisker who?
Is Anne ready? I'm going to whisker away on a special trip.

LAUGHABLE LIST 😆

Signs you have a terrible mountain-climbing guide:
He starts every day's preparation by building snow forts.

She repeatedly asks, "Is it just me or is it chilly up here?"

He uses the oxygen tanks to make balloon animals.

She doesn't pack any food because she's hoping to pick up a burger along the way.

KNOCK! KNOCK!
Who's there?
Manure.
Manure who?
Manure making some awful puns today!

Chitchat

JOSH: **Oh no! My bird escaped its cage!**

DYLAN: **Looks like it used a crow-bar to escape.**

KNOCK! KNOCK!
Who's there?
Buzz.
Buzz who?
Hurry, we're going to mizz our buzz.

Why couldn't the cephalopod focus on its work?

Because its thoughts were octopied.

Chitchat

SURFER 1: **Hey, why are you wearing a baseball mitt?**

SURFER 2: **Because you said we were going to catch some waves.**

Chitchat

LISA: **Hey! Someone stole my recliner!**

FRED: **I couldn't chair less.**

LAUGHABLE LIST
Jobs for dogs:
Barkeologist

Lab technician

Border collie guard

Puppeteer

Pawty planner

KNOCK! KNOCK!
Who's there?
Collie.
Collie who?
Collie you when it's time to take the dogs for a walk.

105

Chitchat

RIKU: **Are you going to watch the fishing competition today?**

KEVIN: **Is it online?**

RIKU: **Yes, but I can't get a good stream.**

Chitchat

BUS DRIVER: **Where to?**

FROG: **I'm heading down to the pond. Mind if I catch a ride?**

BUS DRIVER: **Hop on!**

How do computers cool off?

They open Windows.

106

What kind of makeup do zombie models wear?

Ma-scare-a.

Chitchat

KATHRYN: **Are you all ready for our mountain-climbing trip?**

MELI: **Yep, I'm in peak condition!**

What starts out **tall,** but the longer it stands, the shorter it **grows?**

107

A candle.

KNOCK!
KNOCK!
Who's there?
Paw.
Paw who?
You paw thing.
Have you been inside
all day?

109

Say this fast three times:

Bob bakes batches of bitter brown blueberry bread.

KNOCK!
KNOCK!
Who's there?
Adam.
Adam who?
Up and Adam,
it's time to go!

What do you get if you cross a witch with Rice Krispies?

Snap, cackle, and pop!

Chitchat

ELECTRICIAN'S BOSS: **Wire you insulate?**

ELECTRICIAN: **Watt's it to you?**

What do you call a shark giving presents?

Santa Jaws.

Chitchat

CAMPER: **Shhhhh, please don't talk so loud!**

CAMP LEADER: **Oh! Sorry. What's wrong?**

CAMPER: **I've got a sleeping bag, and I don't want to wake it up!**

How did the scarecrow fix the hole in his pants?

With a pumpkin patch.

What position does the invisible man play on his hockey team?

No one knows.

KNOCK! KNOCK!

Who's there?
Wool.
Wool who?
I wool keep knocking until you open up.

Riddle Me THIS!

What happens once in a minute, twice in a moment, but never in a thousand years?

The letter m.

Snowman illnesses:

Frostbite

Termites (affects twig arms only)

A cold

Snowflakey skin

What kind of cereal does a penguin eat?

Frosted Fish Flakes.

111

Why did the kayaker cross the Atlantic?

To get to the other side.

Riddle Me THIS!

What has armor but doesn't fight and is always home when on the move?

A turtle.

KNOCK! KNOCK!

Who's there?
Dishes.
Dishes who?
Dishes your mother. Did you clean your room?

What kind of cell phone does an optometrist use?

An eye phone.

What do you do if you go on safari and a lion wants to sleep in your tent?

Sleep somewhere else.

Riddle Me THIS!

I don't speak unless spoken to. Many have heard me but none have seen me. What am I?

An echo.

What do scientists use to freshen their breath?

Experi-mints.

What kind of garden does a droid plant?

A bot-anical garden.

What do you call a vampire that eats too many beans?

Count Flatula.

What do you get if you cross a lamb and Japanese food?

Su-sheep.

Chitchat

WAITER: **Welcome to Soul Food, may I take your order?**

GHOST: **I'll have the boo-logna sandwich.**

Riddle Me THIS!

**I dig tiny holes and fill them with silver or gold.
I can also build bridges of silver and crowns of gold.
Sooner or later everyone sees me, but most
are afraid of me. Who am I?**

The dentist.

Say this fast three times:

Turbo sherbet.

Chitchat

PIRATE WITH PEG LEG: **Have you been a pirate all your life?**

ONE-EYED PIRATE: **No, I used to be a teacher, but I got fired.**

PIRATE WITH PEG LEG: **Why?**

ONE-EYED PIRATE: **Because I only had one pupil!**

Why doesn't the computer talk to its parents about work?

Because it makes its mother board.

Riddle Me THIS!

If an electric train is traveling east, but there is a strong wind from the west, which way will the smoke from the train blow?

Electric trains don't produce smoke.

114

Terrible Halloween treats:
Scabby Taffy—pick your favorite flavor.

Taran-chew-las—bite into them before they bite into you!

Pickled Pumpkin Guts—eat till you bust a gut!

Furry Fun Dip—now with 10 percent more hair!

Chitchat

DOOR: **Ugh, my hinges are aching!**

WINDOW: **Stop your squeaking. I'm the one with the pane.**

What kind of fruit has a bad attitude?

A grizzly pear.

Chitchat

MALE DEER: **Oh no, we will never get home now!**

FEMALE DEER: **Why don't we keep going?**

MALE DEER: **Because the buck stops here.**

KNOCK!
KNOCK!
Who's there?
Lobster.
Lobster who?
**Have you seen my mom?
I think I lobster.**

Chitchat

CUSTOMER: **I'm leaving for my cruise, and I need to pick up my laundry.**

DRY CLEANER: **OK, let me just see if I can find it.**

CUSTOMER: **Hurry! Hurry! I don't want to miss my boat.**

DRY CLEANER: **All right, all right, keep your pants on.**

KNOCK!
KNOCK!
Who's there?
Dozen.
Dozen who?
Dozen anyone want to let me in?

LAUGHABLE LIST

Not very scary monsters:
The Toe Tickler

Abominable Sno-Cone

The Sock-Less Monster

Soup-acabra

Chitchat

LARISSA: **I hear our science teacher is a vampire.**

DYLAN: **What?**

LARISSA: **She'll probably give us lots of blood tests.**

Why are writers so logical?

Because they have a lot of comma sense.

Say this fast three times:

The cracked crackers were kept in the cracker shack until they took their crackers back.

Chitchat

POLICE OFFICER: **We caught your dog chasing down people on bikes.**

DOG OWNER: **That's impossible, my dog doesn't even own a bike.**

Where do Canadian sheep come from?

Manito-baa.

Why couldn't the computer take off its baseball hat?

Because the caps lock was on.

Chitchat

GUIDE: **If you look to your left, you'll see a talking giraffe.**

TOURIST: **Wow! He's really talking up a storm.**

GUIDE: **Yes, he's giving a speech on the solar system, but it's kind of hard to hear.**

TOURIST: **Oh well, it's way over my head anyway.**

Riddle Me THIS!

What starts with a *T*, ends with a *T*, and is full of *T*?

A teapot.

Riddle Me THIS!

You can enter, but you can't come in. I can give you space, but no room. I have keys, but no keyholes. What am I?

A computer keyboard.

Why do astronauts look forward to liftoff?

Because it's a blast.

Riddle Me THIS!

Two fathers and two sons go fishing, but there are only three people in the boat. How is this possible?

It was a grandfather, a father, and a son on the fishing trip.

KNOCK!
KNOCK!
Who's there?
Quartz.
Quartz who?
Of quartz I'm here on time!

What do you call it when your fingers are too cold to text properly?

Typo-thermia.

Why can't you call the zoo on the phone?

Because the lion is always busy.

KNOCK!
KNOCK!
Who's there?
Peas.
Peas who?
Peas tell me there are no more knock-knock jokes!

What position does a ghost play on a soccer team?

Ghost-keeper.

What has two claws, four wheels, and a meter?

A taxi-crab.

KNOCK!
KNOCK!
Who's there?
Interrupting cow.
Interrupting—
Moo!!

Say this fast three times:

Beep bob bing bong bananas.

Why was the archaeologist upset?

His job was in ruins.

What kind of jokes do farmers like?

Corny ones.

What kind of bird is always out of breath?

A puffin.

What's the only coat you put on wet?

A coat of paint.

Say this fast three times:

George ignored the boy cyborg.

What time do man-eating monsters wake up?

Ate o'clock.

Why can't you trust graph paper?

Because it's always plotting something.

What do cats listen to on their music players?

Mew-sic.

KNOCK!
KNOCK!
Who's there?
Omelet.
Omelet who?
Omelet that slide ... this time.

What's an Irish setter's favorite holiday?

St. Pawtrick's Day.

Riddle Me THIS!

Three men were on a hike when it started to rain. Only two of them got their hair wet. How is that possible?

The third man was bald.

Why did the orange put on sunscreen?

It didn't want to peel.

Why did the beekeeper go to the doctor?

Because she had hives.

JOKE FINDER

Chitchats

Allison/Diego 67
Alvaro/Kai 104
Asha/Aditya 60
Bob/Doug 69
bus driver/frog 106
camper/camp leader 110
Carrie/Charlotte 8
chef/diner 29
cow 1/cow 2 96
customer/baker 28
customer/dry cleaner 115
customer/pet store owner 77
cutlery 1/cutlery 2 40
David/Lauren 32
diner/waiter 17
dog 1/dog 2 62
door/window 114
Dracula/ghoul 92
duck/skunk 99
electrician's boss/electrician 110
elephant 1/elephant 2 23
Ellen/Jim 84
eye doctor/patient 21
farmer 1/farmer 2 91, 95
fisherman 1/fisherman 2 37
Gary/Nico 74
ghoul/demon 58
gingerbread man/gingerbread
    woman 7
guide/tourist 116
iron 1/iron 2 33
Jeff/Erin 20
Jim/Ellen 7
Josh/Dylan 104
Julia/Cathie 96
Kathryn/Meli 106
kid/woman 5
Larissa/Dylan 115
Lisa/Fred 105
male deer/female deer 114
manager/employee 52
marathon runner/doctor 20

Maria/Wendy 90
Marie/Gary 29
mom/daughter 92
mom cow/calf 75
monster 1/monster 2 84
parakeet 1/parakeet 2 85
patient/doctor 76
pirate with peg leg/one-eyed
    pirate 113
police officer/dog owner 116
porcupine 1/porcupine 2 14
Riku/Kevin 105
robot/lab tech 69
safari tourist/safari guide 47
Sanjida/Priya 100
science teacher/principal 11
skier 1/skier 2 48
statue 1/statue 2 33
student 1/student 2 53
surfer 1/surfer 2 105
Tony/Louise 37
vampire 1/vampire 2 95
vegetable farmer/son 11
waiter/ghost 113
waiter on a cruise ship/
    werewolf 86
writer/editor 93
zookeeper 1/zookeeper 2 85

Knock-knock Jokes

acid 80
Adam 109
Adelia 76
al dente 42
Amos 79
bear claws 90
bed 102
bee 39
bubbly 99
butter 42
butternut 32
buzz 105
cannoli 6
canoe 40
cashew 81

chicken 85
classify 100
collie 105
cook 99
crumb 104
dishes 111
dozen 115
fangs 68
filter 18
foal 12
frappé 102
Havana 83
herd 53
hive 60
Hugo 33
Ida 72
iguana 6
interrupting cow 120
ivory 50
Jamaican 43
Julian 59
kanga 82
kitten 13
latte 101
letters 4
llama 43
loafing 95
lobster 115
manure 104
naan 8
nacho 90
neon 24
nickel 79
ogre 43
omelet 122
ooze 42
owl 102
pasta 22
paw 109
peas 120
pollen 52
pun 12
quack 94
quartz 120
queso 49

safari 84
Sam 13
sand 27
Santa 71
scold 93
scone 63
shave 101
shell 49
snow 82
some fin 73
squidding 70
swarm 63
swimmer 30
taco 91
tennis 60
voodoo 68
Wader 33
water 14
weirdo 93
wheat 38
whisker 104
wire 39
woo 58
wool 110
yeast 10
zombies 91

Laughable Lists

animal Valentine's Day cards 57
books by robot authors 95
crazy campsites 7
jobs for dogs 105
lesser known landmarks 24
new dog breeds 78
not very scary monsters 115
pig party games 68
signs there's a hole in your pool 19
signs you have a terrible
   mountain-climbing guide 104
signs you have an old computer 31
signs you're in a bad motel 94
snowman illnesses 111
terrible Halloween treats 114
terrible safari advertisements 92

Question-and-Answer

aardvark 21
Abominable Snowman 74
alligators 23
amnesia 39
ape 42, 62
archaeologist 121
archers 70
artists 13, 43
astronauts 59, 119
baker 21, 53, 103
barbecue 102
barber 52, 75
baseball 8, 92, 116
basketball 20, 23, 64, 92
batteries 71, 81, 85
bee 24
beekeeper 123
Bigfoot 58, 78, 89
biologist 37, 68
birds 18, 38, 39, 58, 121
blood bank 43
bread 53, 83, 84, 89
bridges 49, 57
broom 48, 85
bubblegum 62
bugs 79, 89
buses 72, 80
camping 72, 90
Canada 73, 95, 116
canary 9
carpenter 67
cars 12, 39, 52, 68, 84, 85, 103
cats 22, 28, 41, 51, 52, 72, 74, 93, 122
cephalopod 105
cereal 110, 111
chandelier 13
cheese 22, 59
chemist 93
chickens 19, 20, 64, 74, 83
coffee beans 77
colds 23, 101
comedian 84

computer programmers 12, 60
computers 7, 11, 30, 33, 34, 37, 41, 92, 106, 114, 116
cookies 24, 43, 103
corn 51
cows 49, 54, 64
creek 69
cruise ship 42
cupcake 52
dance 11, 13, 90
Darth Vader 28
dentist 22, 30, 50
dinosaur 2–3, 48, 75
doctor 41, 43, 123
dogs 37, 42, 43, 48, 68, 73, 74, 78, 81, 123
Dracula 20
droid 112
eggs 12, 79
elephant 22, 28
fangs 7, 32, 84
farmers 72, 121
ferret 40, 83
fish 20, 44, 58, 59, 81, 85
fishermen 76
fishing lure 82
flashlight 81
fleas 12, 53
flower 13
flu 61
fog 69
font 10
football 54
fountain of youth 14
French fries 23, 47
frogs 5, 60
fruit 13, 34, 57, 61, 62, 86, 114
garden 33, 112
geologists 27
ghosts 17, 37, 43, 44, 50, 53, 74, 78, 90, 91, 96, 120
ghoul 94
giraffe 67
goat 51
Godzilla 49

JOKE FINDER

graph paper 122
green 31, 33, 51, 102
grizzly bear 13
guinea pig 10
guitarists 27, 101
gymnasts 96
Halloween 32
hamburgers 13, 23
hedgehogs 4, 64, 67
hockey 54, 110
holiday 43, 75, 123
horses 40, 62
hot dog 42, 100
hot dog bun 19, 72
insect 20, 32, 69, 85
invisible man 40, 110
jaguar 70
jailer 72
jellyfish 14
jeweler 72
kayakers 59, 111
kittens 17, 18, 84
knight 63
ladders 19
lambs 63, 112
leech 74
letters 75, 80
lion 112, 120
lobster 4
lunch 13, 22, 86
magician 78
magnet 64
medicine 17
mice 58, 72, 77

money 20, 75, 76
monkeys 12, 23, 32, 53, 89
monsters 18, 24, 59, 70, 122
muffin 38, 52
music 10, 42, 72, 95, 122
musical instrument 44, 71
musicians 69, 83
nut 31
opera singer 84
oranges 62, 82, 86, 123
paint 121
pencil 38
penguins 75, 111
pepper 34
petri dishes 78
pharmacy 61
phone 9, 29, 47, 112, 120
pickle 22
pie 44, 62
piemakers 31
pigs 31, 33, 54, 73, 94, 103
pirate 80
pizza 21
planets 12
polar bears 13, 34, 61
potato chip 23, 79
print shop 94
pumpkin 71, 110
puppies 30, 59, 60
rabbits 9, 41, 49
race-car drivers 69
races 11, 31, 52, 62, 78, 100
rhinoceros 86
river 69
robot 12, 71, 79, 86
rodent 13, 58

safari 112
sardine 79
scarecrow 86, 110
scientists 100, 112
scuba divers 75
seashore 59
shark 110
sheep 12, 52, 112, 116
shoemaker 22
shoes 23, 37
shrimp 48
skeletons 21, 95, 104
skydiving 23, 38, 39
snails 84
snakes 12, 34, 50, 82
snowmen 44
snowsuit 81
soccer 75, 120
soft drinks 40, 72, 79
spiders 5, 6
statue 48
steak 14
students 6, 10, 12, 27
sumo wrestlers 69
sun 76
superhero 48
sweaters 34, 58, 61
Tarzan 17
taxis 29, 120
teacher 23, 27, 61, 80
tennis 44, 71
texting 120
toilet 22
tornado 68
trampoline 82
travel 6, 41, 53
trees 10, 43, 74, 82, 90
turtle 4, 40, 84
Valentine's Day 30, 53
vampires 7, 79, 85, 112
weasel family 52
werewolf 80
windshield 79
witches 48, 68, 75, 92, 110
writers 115

We promised

591 ½ jokes,

so here's the last ½.
(You finish it!)

How do you
keep a camel
in suspense?

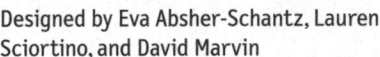

Random House Children's Books
A division of Penguin Random House LLC
1745 Broadway, New York, NY 10019
penguinrandomhouse.com
rhcbooks.com

Designed by Eva Absher-Schantz, Lauren
Sciortino, and David Marvin

Book team: Kathryn Williams, editor; Melissa
Santoyo, editorial assistant; Lori Epstein,
photo director; Colin Wheeler, photo editor;
Molly Reid, production editor; Yogi Carroll,
production manager; Lauren Sciortino,
associate designer.

Library of Congress Cataloging-in-Publication
Data is available upon request.
ISBN 978-1-4263-7805-8 (trade paperback) —
ISBN 978-1-4263-7804-1 (lib. bdg.)

Manufactured in the United States
1st Printing

The authorized representative in the EU for
product safety and compliance is Penguin
Random House Ireland, Morrison Chambers,
32 Nassau Street, Dublin D02 YH68, Ireland,
https://eu-contact.penguin.ie.

x-ray technician 74
x-rays 30
zombies 86, 95, 106
zoo 120

Riddle Me This!

bald man 123
baseball team 22
bottle 35–36
candle 107–108
computer keyboard 119
dentist 113
dog 103
echo 112
egg 87–88
electric train 114
fishing trip 119
goose 15–16
Grand Canyon 97–98
haunted house 11
horse 65–66
kangaroo 25–26
letter *m* 111
running 9

shadow 103
skydiving school 55–56
stamp 45–46
teapot 117–118
turtle 111

Tongue Twisters

aardvark 18
baboon 30
balloon 14
bananas 121
biscuit mixer 32
Bob 109
Brian 74
bulb 9
cheese 102
chop shops 51
crackers 115
cummerbund 53
elves 32
fillies 73
film festival 17
firefighters 14
fish sauce shop 100

flapjacks 4
frogs 89
George 121
ghosts 21
haunted houses 89
kitties 85
llamas 94
Philip 10
rapids 6
rascals 85
Rosie 28
salary 52
Santa 33
selfie 103
sharks 23
shellfish 52
sherbet 113
ship trips 53
shoes 8
skunk 33
Slurpees 102
snakes 10, 100
tree toad 30
watches 74

127

Illustration Credits:

Abbreviations: AS = Adobe Stock; SS = Shutterstock
Cover: (background), alphaspirit/AS; (UP), Elena Sherengovskaya/SS; (LO), Rita Kochmarjova/AS; Spine: Rita Kochmarjova/AS; (pattern throughout), Nattle/SS; (pattern throughout), Gorbash Varvara/SS; (pattern throughout), troyka/SS; Back cover: asawinimages/SS; 3 (lemon), Iurii Stepanov/SS; 6-7, patrimonio designs ltd/SS; 9 (bird), mhatzapa/SS; 10 (guinea pig), HPK Design Studio/AS; 10 (snake), Drawlab19/SS; 11, Rashad Ashur/SS; 13, mhatzapa/SS; 14 (porcupines), lineartestpilot/AS; 14 (hat), Artist_inspirer/AS; 14 (porcupines), lineartestpilot/AS; 14 (jellyfish), mhatzapa/SS; 17 (ghost), SK Photographer-Vector/SS; 17 (flowers), redchocolatte/AS; 20, SK Photographer-Vector/SS; 21, Klara Viskova/AS; 22, Melody A/SS; 23, kosmofish/SS; 24, Katsiaryna Pleshakova/SS; 25-26, kronalux/AS; 27 (sunglasses), fosin/SS; 27 (guitar), Paul Kovaloff/AS; 27 (music), Martial Red/SS; 28-29, Robert Adrian Hillman/SS; 31, insima/SS; 32, Elena Pimukova/SS; 37, Zhuko/SS; 38 (skydiver), BlueRingMedia/SS; 38 (goose), oorka/SS; 39, michalsanca/AS; 40, mhatzapa/SS; 41, Natasha Pankina/SS; 42, Igor/AS; 44 (pie), Olga/AS; 44 (wings), liubov/AS; 45-46, Fuadi Alhusaini/AS; 48, inspiring.team/AS; 49, asantosg/AS; 50, Nadzin/AS; 51, jan stopka/AS; 55-56, Elena/AS; 58 (truck), Draco77/AS; 59 (astronaut), vectorpouch/AS; 59 (fork), grgroup/AS; 60, mark/AS; 61 (pear texture), Obsessively/AS; 64 (chicken), FutureFFX/AS; 64 (cow), Shallu Narula/SS; 65-66, Vector Tradition/AS; 67 (hedgehog), bartamarabara/AS; 67 (toothbrush), nazar12/AS; 68 (tornado), NWM/AS; 69 (flute), mo-ment/AS; 69 (robot), vectorchef/AS; 70 (squid), KVasay/AS; 71 (guitars), metelsky25/AS; 71 (tuba), Fabien/AS; 73, zolotons/AS; 75, Janna Mudrak/AS; 77, Satoru Sketches/AS; 78, Vector Deluxe Studio/AS; 79, anatolir/AS; 80, sonia_ai/AS; 81, blumer1979/AS; 82, Matthew/AS; 83 (ferret), insima/AS; 83 (music), Neo/AS; 85, CreativeDesigns/AS; 87-88, RobbinLee/AS; 89 (ghosts), Nadzin/AS; 89 (Bigfoot), Zilvinas/AS; 90, Lugostock/AS; 91, aksol/AS; 92, Iryna Palmina/SS; 93, Dadan_pm/SS; 94, Evgeny Turaev/SS; 95, SK Photographer-Vector/SS; 96, AlexeyGorchakov/SS; 97-98, Viktoriia_Patapova/SS; 99 (birds), mhatzapa/SS; 99 (cloud), Elena Pimukova/SS; 99 (bird), Elena Pimukova/SS; 100 (rabbit), Sko Helen/SS; 100 (snake), Drawlab19/SS; 101 (coffee), mhatzapa/SS; 101 (guitars), Elena Pimukova/SS; 103 (texture), abeadev/AS; 104, 6x6x6/SS; 105, CarrotStudios/AS; 106 (zombie), SK Photographer-Vector/SS; 106 (computer), dandoo/SS; 106 (topography), biancaoddi/AS; 107-108, Flying Master/SS; 111, Shum-stock/SS; 112, Ksenya Savva/SS; 113 (tooth A), callmefiz/SS; 113 (tooth B), callmefiz/SS; 114 (deer), Sko Helen/SS; 117-118, SkillUp/SS; 119 (astronaut A), Catalyst Labs/SS; 119 (astronaut B), Catalyst Labs/SS; 122, I Kadek Yogi Pranata/SS; 123 (bees), smilewithjul/SS; 123 (dog), Igor Zakowski/SS